His Greatness

by Daniel MacIvor

Playwrights Canada Press
Toronto • Canada

Playwrights Canada Press
The Canadian Drama Publisher
215 Spadina Avenue, Suite 230, Toronto, Ontario CANADA M5T 2C7
416-703-0013 fax 416-408-3402
orders@playwrightscanada.com • www.playwrightscanada.com

This book would be twice its cover price were it not for the support of Canadian taxpayers through the Government of Canada Book Publishing Industry Development Programme, the Canada Council for the Arts, the Ontario Arts Council and the Ontario Media Development Corporation.

Cover Design JLArt and Daniel MacIvor
Production Editor: JLArt

Library and Archives Canada Cataloguing in Publication

MacIvor, Daniel, 1962-
    His greatness / Daniel MacIvor.

A play.
ISBN 978-0-88754-829-1

    1. Williams, Tennessee, 1911-1983--Drama. I. Title.

PS8575.I86H58 2008   C812'.54   C2008-903215-2

First edition: July 2008.
Printed and bound by AGMV Marquis at Quebec, Canada.

For Danny

Charles Gallant
photo by David Cooper Photography

Foreword

My relationship with Tennessee Williams began when I was in high school and read *The Glass Menagerie* as taught by my grade 12 English teacher Miss Donaldson. She was tiny and solid and known for her stern ways: penmanship was paramount, grammar was holy and boorish behaviour was never, ever tolerated. This was reflected by her nickname— "Donaldson"—not some childish take on a physical attribute, ("Shorty"), not her perceived personality ("The Hammer"), but just "Donaldson"— and spoken in tones as a private might refer to a sergeant or a general: "Who'd you get for English next year?" "Donaldson." "Oh, man, that's rough," might go the dialogue. She was also one of those English teachers who loved, from deep, deep within her stern and solid soul, drama. In class when we read the play we were studying aloud she would take a role herself—her Lady McB was blood-curdlingly good. Considering her choice of role in Shakespeare and the image she projected, one might imagine that she would take on Amanda when reading *Menagerie* but no, instead she became Laura. It was a remarkable thing to watch as she walked slowly up and down the aisles of the classroom, book in hand, this formidable woman turning all soft and sweet and lost and broken. With Shakespeare I felt it was Donaldson who was bringing out her own rage and ambition and fortitude in the character, but with Laura it was something else that was doing this to her. It was the writing. This was some kind of magic happening. And this brokenness was not only hers but mine, and not only mine but the writer's.

Some years later, working as a young actor at the Stephenville Festival in Newfoundland under the mentorship of the late great theatre empresario Maxim Mazumdar—a massive Williams afficionado— I became familiar with the larger body of Tennessee's work: the short stories, the unseen one-acts, the surreal experimental plays, which from Maxim's personal bookshelves I devoured over a few days the way one might a dead man's diaries, searching for some secret. There was something going on here, some common thread beyond theme, beyond the writer's intention, but I couldn't put my finger on it.

Then, in 1988 I had the great fortune of playing Tom in Martin Kinch's production of *The Glass Menagerie* at Theatre Calgary. It was while deep inside the play, that I figured out what I identified with in all the work of this man—brokenness. All of the characters in *Menagerie* were broken, even the Gentleman Caller seemed like he was destined to a mediocre life of middling dreams realized. And past *Menagerie* even, who wasn't broken? Blanche, Stanley and Stella in *Streetcar*? Check. Maxine and Rev. Shannon in *Iguana*? Check. Catherine in *Suddenly*? Check. Brick, Maggie and even Big Daddy in *Cat*? Check and check and check. But the real revelation to me was that, not only were the characters broken, the plays themselves were broken. These plays were not slick, smooth easy rides—confidently built from clear thought—but rather confused and questioning and contradictory. Just like life, just like us.

Again later, in the mid-90s, a good friend of mine told a few of us at a party a first hand account of his dark days in Vancouver and a meeting he had with Tennessee when Williams was there for the opening of his "new" play *The Red Devil Battery Sign* (and if you can find me a more broken play than this from a major playwright... oh well, there is *Camino Real*). The story was vivid and shocking and the archetypal portrait of a broken man. Such a heartbreaking and darkly poetic tale it inspired my friend and fellow party-goer, Sky Gilbert, to write his dark and poetic one-act play *My Night With Tennessee*. It was a story I continued to hear in different forms and from many people for years. It was the theatre practitioners' cautionary tale. Just the way we like it, sordid and beautiful.

In 2005 I was asked to write a play to be workshopped at Encore Theatre in San Francisco. I was in the midst of great personal and professional turmoil—I had just ended a twenty-year run as a partner in a successful theatre company and I was battling a few dark and poetic demons of my own. When I sat down to consider writing, I asked myself what did I need to write about now? I thought about legacy. I thought about success and failure. I thought about my plays. I looked closely at them from an unbiased—but admittedly less than sunny—perspective. In my plays there was always something unplayable, too real, too poetic, too trying for something and just missing it, too wanting love and rejecting it. Where my plays succeeded was ultimately where they failed, their inarticulateness, their feeling too old-fashioned while trying to be "modern," their inability to be smooth and slick and easy while trying so desperately for exactly those qualities. This is where the plays felt human, it was the audience's way into them. How the plays were broken, was how I was broken, was how we are broken. Suddenly I felt a deep connection with Williams, and I remembered that Vancouver story. Thus began *His Greatness*.

His Greatness is not a play about Tennessee Williams. Reading or viewing this play will not give one insight in the man who was born

Thomas Lanier Williams and became the great American playwright who called himself Tennessee. It will not shed light on his relationship to his family or the reasons for his work. It will not have you closing the book or leaving the theatre saying, "Oh, so that explains why he...." *His Greatness* is a play about three lost men who have forgotten their dream of a life, and as a result of the events of two days come to remember, if not their dream, at least that they once had a dream. It is a play about three gay men living fully and openly in the world of the early 80s, just before everything was about to change forever. It is a play about three broken men who, because of their time together, realize that perhaps by leaving, by stopping, by starting again there is maybe a chance to be fixed. In his forward to *Sweet Bird of Youth* Tennessee said, "I cannot expose a human weakness on the stage unless I know it through having it myself." In that respect *His Greatness* is, in its deepest, most flawed and weakest heart, a play about me. And if you are anything like me at all, it is a play about you.

DM

Acknowledgements

Many thanks to all those who helped me with the development of this play, especially Lisa Steindler at Encore Theatre in San Francisco, Andrey Tarasiuk at the Stratford Festival, Bill Millerd and all at the Arts Club in Vancouver, Frances Hill at Urban Stages in New York, Mary Colin Chisholm, Christian Murray, Gordon White, John Dartt and Kathryn MacLellan who participated in the reading at Neptune Theatre in Halifax, my agent Thomas Pearson, my dear friends Brad Horvath, Guntar Kravis, Emmy Alcorn and Kim Purtell, the brilliant and beautiful Linda Moore and most especially to Rob Jansen and Ashley Gates for your belief and love and friendship.

His Greatness was first produced by the Arts Club Theatre, Vancouver, B.C., October 11–November 10, 2007 with the following company:

PLAYWRIGHT	Allan Gray
ASSISTANT	David Marr
YOUNG MAN	Charles Gallant
JULIE *(voice-over)*	Medina Hahn
CAROLE *(voice-over)*	Emma Lancaster

Director: Linda Moore
Scenery Design: Kevin McAllistar
Lighting Design: Alan Brodie
Costume Design: Angela Bright
Production Dramaturge: Rachel Ditor
Stage Manager: Allison Spearin
Assistant Stage Manager: Robin Bancroft-Wilson

• • •

His Greatness was first presented in a staged workshop in 2006, produced by Montsgo Projects, New York, New York and Encore Theater, San Francisco, California at the Thick House Theatre, San Francisco.
Playwright: Daniel MacIvor, Assistant: Michael Sommers, Young Man: Ian Scott McGregor. Directed by Daniel MacIvor, designed by Robert Jansen, assistant directed by Ashley Gates.

• • •

In 2007 *His Greatness* was presented in a staged reading workshop at the Stratford Festival.
Playwright: Richard Monette, Assistant: Steve Cumyn, Young Man: Allan Hawco. Directed by Linda Moore.

Characters

PLAYWRIGHT
ASSISTANT
YOUNG MAN
JULIE *(voice-over)*
CAROLE *(voice-over)*

His Greatness

PROLOGUE

In the black, the face of an older man. He is the PLAYWRIGHT. He speaks to the audience.

PLAYWRIGHT
There you are, still and silent. Waiting. Believing that I will have something to say. All I have to offer now is my life, or what's left of it. It wasn't always like this. In the beginning there was no end to the ideas. And as different as they were and as many as they were, they would always come to my mind in the same fashion. First the empty stage. And what would come next was light, qualities of light: morning, late afternoon, the glow of a red neon sign outside the window, moonlight through the leaves of a cottonwood tree. Then in the light would become visible the objects of a world: a doorway, then a window, perhaps a bed, an exit stage left, a table stage right. And next came the bodies made flesh from the fractured voices in my head. The young man distraught in a corner, the fading beauty facing out, looking over her shoulder, clutching at a memory. And then the words would come with all their wit and insight and twisted passion. And from the words would come the story, rushing like a river, pulling me along with it, an ancient river, like it had been there all the time just waiting to be named. But that was the beginning and now here we are in a place that must be near the end, because the river now runs dry, the voices are silent. The stage is dark.

ACT ONE

SCENE ONE   Thursday Afternoon

The stage is dark. A spent, but handsome, man in his forties enters, crossing through the darkness. He is the ASSISTANT.

ASSISTANT
Rise and shine.

PLAYWRIGHT
What?

ASSISTANT
Get up.

PLAYWRIGHT
Is it morning already?

ASSISTANT
Actually it's the middle of the afternoon.

The ASSISTANT opens the curtains of a large window. Bright light.

We are in the bedroom of a hotel suite in Vancouver, Canada, November of 1980. This is the best room in a fading downtown hotel. There is door stage right which leads to the offstage sitting room and main hallway door. A king-sized bed takes up the centre of the room, to the left of the bed is a door to the partially visible bathroom. On the left wall is a large window which, beyond the curtains, looks out onto an unseen parking lot. Across the room, a mirror. The room aspires to a kind of grandeur which it manages when the lights are low enough, but when the lights are bright we see the ghosts of many sad lives lived here. The room is in great disarray from last night's party and throughout the scene the ASSISTANT goes about restoring it to perfection.

PLAYWRIGHT
(reacting to the light) Now that's just cruel.

ASSISTANT
It's something called "day," have you heard of it?

PLAYWRIGHT
My eyes!

ASSISTANT
Am I blinding you with this horrible light? Is the daylight unnecessary? That's what it was yesterday. "The unnecessary daylight." You really should write that stuff down.

PLAYWRIGHT
I'd gladly take unnecessary if it meant I'd get something for this horrible pain.

ASSISTANT
Which pain?

PLAYWRIGHT
The pain in my soul.

ASSISTANT
That's not your soul, it's your hangover.

PLAYWRIGHT
Where are we?

ASSISTANT
Do we have to start every day like this?

PLAYWRIGHT
Humour me.

ASSISTANT
A hotel suite in Vancouver.

PLAYWRIGHT
That's different. And Vancouver is where?

ASSISTANT
A city in a country north of Seattle.

PLAYWRIGHT
Who's the president?

ASSISTANT
They don't have a president, they have a prime minister, and he's usually somebody French.

PLAYWRIGHT
Is it still 1980?

ASSISTANT
Just a couple of months of it left.

PLAYWRIGHT
And who am I?

ASSISTANT
The Famous American Playwright.

PLAYWRIGHT
(mocking) "Famous." Like I give a rat's ass about such things.

ASSISTANT
No, you don't care about that.

PLAYWRIGHT
Exactly.

ASSISTANT
I was being ironic.

PLAYWRIGHT
My dear, irony is well out of your reach, it requires wit.

ASSISTANT
We're starting early.

PLAYWRIGHT
"Famous." Famous is for starlets and television actors. I prefer something with a little more dignity.

ASSISTANT
Celebrated?

PLAYWRIGHT
Eminent. Our Most Eminent American Playwright.

ASSISTANT
Maybe.

PLAYWRIGHT
You argue?

ASSISTANT
Some might.

PLAYWRIGHT
Who's arguing?

ASSISTANT
Arthur Miller for one.

PLAYWRIGHT

Oh, is that horrible son of a bitch still alive?

ASSISTANT

Generous.

PLAYWRIGHT

I mean, really. That play about the witches, I mean, that's just too easy. And what kind of name is Happy, I mean, that's just pushing the envelope past the postman with your nose. I could have had Marilyn you know.

ASSISTANT

You should write that.

PLAYWRIGHT

Write what?

ASSISTANT

Your Marilyn stories.

PLAYWRIGHT

I don't write about my life.

ASSISTANT

Of course.

PLAYWRIGHT

And you are?

ASSISTANT

The nursemaid.

PLAYWRIGHT

Oh, please.

ASSISTANT

The once and former muse.

PLAYWRIGHT

Aren't you poetic.

ASSISTANT

That used to be your job.

PLAYWRIGHT

How did last night end up?

ASSISTANT
What's the last thing you remember?

PLAYWRIGHT
The gay one was looking for a bottle.

ASSISTANT
He's one of the designers and he's not gay.

PLAYWRIGHT
Oh, please, I can spot a delicate man at fifty paces.

ASSISTANT
He's not. He told you that. And the director told you that.

PLAYWRIGHT
The director was here?

ASSISTANT
Yes.

PLAYWRIGHT
Was I good?

ASSISTANT
You got a little messy after your Warren Beatty speech.

PLAYWRIGHT
I don't make "speeches."

ASSISTANT
The Warren Beatty is becoming a speech.

PLAYWRIGHT
The Warren Beatty's not a speech, it's a story.

ASSISTANT
At seven minutes it's a speech.

PLAYWRIGHT
What about your Julie Christie? I clocked that in at nine minutes once.

ASSISTANT
Julie Christie deserves half an hour. Julie Christie's delicious.

PLAYWRIGHT
"Delicious"?

ASSISTANT

I can appreciate a woman.

PLAYWRIGHT

My dear that's just embarrassing considering that it would be clear to the blind that you'd rather wear a dress than chase one.

ASSISTANT

I've never worn a dress in my life.

PLAYWRIGHT

Figuratively my dear. I don't know about lately but you certainly have taken the feminine role.

ASSISTANT

Regardless, you were giving the Warren Beatty as you were trying to get Robbie in the sack.

PLAYWRIGHT

Robbie?

ASSISTANT

The designer.

PLAYWRIGHT

Oh, yes.

ASSISTANT

And he got mad and then you tried to seduce the director.

PLAYWRIGHT

Oh, yes, that was the director, all right, I'm with you now. What happened after that?

ASSISTANT

Then the director got mad, everybody left.

PLAYWRIGHT

What'd he get mad for?

ASSISTANT

Because you kept saying he was gay.

PLAYWRIGHT

Well he was.

ASSISTANT

No he wasn't.

PLAYWRIGHT
Oh, please, the only pussy he ever had would have been furry and purring in his lap.

ASSISTANT
That's what you said last night.

PLAYWRIGHT
I only speak the truth I see.

The ASSISTANT steps into the bathroom.

So in a nutshell it was a good night.

ASSISTANT
(off) We've had worse.

PLAYWRIGHT
Yes I miss those.

The ASSISTANT returns.

ASSISTANT
Why are all the towels on the floor in the bathroom?

PLAYWRIGHT
I find the bare floor painful on my metabolic arthritis.

ASSISTANT
It's called gout.

PLAYWRIGHT
"Gout" sounds like the affliction of a labourer, or a crusty old invalid. Sounds like something you pick up in a cheap hotel in Times Square.

ASSISTANT
And if you could've got it there you would've.

PLAYWRIGHT
"Gout" is so vile sounding. I am sensitive to words.

The ASSISTANT laughs.

What?

ASSISTANT
Maybe that's why you're not writing anymore. You're allergic to words.

PLAYWRIGHT
I'm not writing because I'm busy with my teaching.

ASSISTANT
"Teaching."

PLAYWRIGHT
Teaching is a noble profession.

ASSISTANT
Not when you can get so drunk doing it you shit your pants.

PLAYWRIGHT
Stop that.

ASSISTANT
I had to change you.

PLAYWRIGHT
Once.

ASSISTANT
That you remember.

PLAYWRIGHT
What?

ASSISTANT
Nothing. Get yourself together—they'll be calling for the interview in few minutes.

The ASSISTANT steps into the bathroom.

PLAYWRIGHT
What interview?

ASSISTANT
The telephone interview with the radio.

PLAYWRIGHT
I won't be talking on any dirty telephone.

ASSISTANT
I had them bring up a speakerphone.

The PLAYWRIGHT takes a bottle from under the covers and pours himself a drink.

PLAYWRIGHT
I'll never understand how people can do that, God knows who from all over wherever and whatnot, talking into that thing, and then people just putting it up there by their mouth like that.

ASSISTANT
You've had a few worse wherevers or whatnots near your mouth.

The ASSISTANT steps back into the room.

Daytime drinking?

PLAYWRIGHT
I know, I know.

ASSISTANT
Is it London again already?

PLAYWRIGHT
No.

The ASSISTANT takes the drink from the PLAYWRIGHT.

ASSISTANT
I'm not doing London again. You lying on the floor of the bathroom with a straw up your nose and a hustler passed out in the bathtub. And me running around London at four in the morning trying to find nasal spray.

PLAYWRIGHT
Nasal spray saved my life.

ASSISTANT
Next time you won't be so lucky.

PLAYWRIGHT
Is that a wish or a prediction?

ASSISTANT
And not even showing up at the opening.

PLAYWRIGHT
Let it go.

ASSISTANT
My mother came.

PLAYWRIGHT
How was I supposed to know your mother was in London.

ASSISTANT
You spoke. We had dinner.

PLAYWRIGHT
We had dinner?

ASSISTANT
Twice! I'm not doing London again. I won't do it. I'll leave.

PLAYWRIGHT
I said it's not going to be London.

ASSISTANT
Or worse, maybe I'll just stay and go to hell right along with you.

PLAYWRIGHT
It won't be London. I'll walk the line. A tentative gait on a narrow line, but I will walk it.

> *The PLAYWRIGHT conciliatorily hands the bottle to the ASSISTANT. The ASSISTANT takes it.*
>
> *After a moment.*

Another day begins?

ASSISTANT
Seems so.

PLAYWRIGHT
And what's the scenario we shall concern ourselves with today? Something tragic perhaps? Will the assistant finally realize that after all these years the playwright has lost his greatness?

ASSISTANT
The only scenario His Greatness better concern himself with is getting his fat ass out of bed.

PLAYWRIGHT
Oh, does this bed make my behind look fat?

ASSISTANT
You're showing up for these people.

PLAYWRIGHT
I know I know.

ASSISTANT
Shameful, missing the preview last night.

PLAYWRIGHT
We were late that's all.

ASSISTANT
It was over! How do you think that made me look?

PLAYWRIGHT
Made you look?

ASSISTANT
I'm supposed to get you where you're supposed to be, that's my job.

PLAYWRIGHT
When did that become your job?

ASSISTANT
When you stopped caring.

PLAYWRIGHT
I care. I care deeply. I wouldn't be here if I didn't care.

ASSISTANT
You wouldn't be here if I didn't pour you onto the goddamn plane.

PLAYWRIGHT
They didn't want me there anyway last night, they were relieved.

ASSISTANT
You only do what you want to do.

PLAYWRIGHT
Well that just seems like common sense to me.

ASSISTANT
Everybody doesn't have it that easy.

PLAYWRIGHT
You think it's easy to write a play?

ASSISTANT
As if you'd remember.

A moment.

PLAYWRIGHT
How's your room?

ASSISTANT
Fine. Tiny. Fine.

PLAYWRIGHT
I think there's a pullout in the sitting room if you might find it more comfortable.

ASSISTANT
I'm fine.

A moment. The ASSISTANT looks out the window.

PLAYWRIGHT
How do I look?

The ASSISTANT looks briefly.

ASSISTANT
Surprisingly handsome. Shockingly. Luckily.

PLAYWRIGHT
How's the view?

ASSISTANT
Parking lot.

PLAYWRIGHT
We've come terribly down in the world haven't we.

ASSISTANT
We met in a parking lot.

PLAYWRIGHT
We met at dinner.

ASSISTANT
We got together in a parking lot.

PLAYWRIGHT
But we met at dinner.

ASSISTANT
We didn't actually "meet" until no money was exchanged.

The PLAYWRIGHT laughs uproariously.

The phone rings. The ASSISTANT answers it.

Yes? Yes. And you are? …Hello, Julie. Here he is.

The ASSISTANT pushes a button on the phone to open the speaker.

JULIE
(*voice-over*) Hello?

PLAYWRIGHT
Well hello, my dear. Are we live to air?

JULIE
(*voice-over*) No no, we'll be taping and then airing around six tonight.

PLAYWRIGHT
Well I must be sure to tune in, I can't wait to hear what I'm going to have to say.

The ASSISTANT gives the PLAYWRIGHT the thumbs up.

JULIE
(*voice-over*) I won't take much of your time, I'll do the intro later.

PLAYWRIGHT
I have heard that I need no introduction.

JULIE
(*voice-over*) And before we start I just want to say I'm a huge fan.

PLAYWRIGHT
(*miming yawning to the ASSISTANT*) Oh, thank you.

JULIE
(*voice-over*) And the play's the talk of the town.

The PLAYWRIGHT gestures "well well" to the ASSISTANT.

Ready…. And…. We'll start just after the music.

PLAYWRIGHT
Of course.

Music. The PLAYWRIGHT mocks the music.

JULIE
(*voice-over*) Welcome to Vancouver.

PLAYWRIGHT
Why thank you. I have never before visited your glorious city, and I must say that is an error on my part that I'm thrilled to have remedied.

JULIE

(*voice-over*) So this is not a new play. Why—

PLAYWRIGHT

Oh, yes, it's a new play.

JULIE

(*voice-over*) But this version was produced in London last year.

The ASSISTANT gestures to the PLAYWRIGHT to say "no."

PLAYWRIGHT

No no no.

The ASSISTANT gestures to the PLAYWRIGHT to say "yes."

But yes, but…

The ASSISTANT gestures to the PLAYWRIGHT: "working on details."

I was working on the play. This is the official version. I didn't even see the play in London.

The ASSISTANT covers his face with his hands.

JULIE

(*voice-over*) You weren't in London?

PLAYWRIGHT

I didn't say I wasn't—I am here now. Let's discuss that.

JULIE

(*voice-over*) Oh, good, all right. Always of great interest are your female characters—

PLAYWRIGHT

(*interrupting*) Indeed, I was raised in a world of women. My father, my grandfather, my brother, they were important players in my early story, but the women took the leading roles: my mother, my beloved grandmother, my darling sister. I was permitted entry to a world most men can only hope to view from a distance. I, too, was an observer but more properly, an intimate observer. I see it in this fashion—

JULIE

(*voice-over*) What do you say to critics who contend that these women are broad strokes? Caricatures? That they're not real women?

PLAYWRIGHT

It's not real, my dear. It's poetry.

JULIE

(voice-over) When you premiered this version in London last year the critics said—

> *The ASSISTANT gestures "stop the interview" to the PLAYWRIGHT. The PLAYWRIGHT ignores the ASSISTANT.*

—that the play was an attempt for you to enter the modern world but in essence it was an old-fashioned play. How do you respond to that?

> *The ASSISTANT gestures "that's been covered" to the PLAYWRIGHT.*

PLAYWRIGHT

It wasn't this play. This is a new play. And I don't need to "enter" the modern world, I am in the modern world. I helped create the modern world. What is "modern"? Tell me that. The human heart is not modern anymore? Longing, love, loss? No? What's a "modern play"?

JULIE

(voice-over) I'm sorry I don't mean to—

PLAYWRIGHT

And that will be all.

> *The PLAYWRIGHT presses buttons to hang up the telephone. We can still hear JULIE through the speaker.*

JULIE

(voice-over) I hope I didn't—I mean no disrespect, I'm just curious about—

PLAYWRIGHT

(to the ASSISTANT) Hang this goddamn thing up.

> *The ASSISTANT pushes a button, hanging up the phone.*
>
> *Silence as the PLAYWRIGHT rises and makes his way with some delicate difficulty to the bottle of whiskey and pours himself a glass. He takes a drink. After a moment.*

I'm not modern?

ASSISTANT
    (gently) What does she know.

      The PLAYWRIGHT finishes his drink and pours himself another.

PLAYWRIGHT
    What am I now, a dinosaur? Goddamn New York. Those awful little brutish dramas with their three-word lines barked by barbarians.

ASSISTANT
    (kindly) You've written a barbarian or two in your time.

PLAYWRIGHT
    "In my time"? Really. My time is up is it?

      A moment of silence.

ASSISTANT
    You could have just said—

PLAYWRIGHT
    An awful girl.

ASSISTANT
    You should have told her that bit about fixing up the old plays.

PLAYWRIGHT
    What "bit"?

ASSISTANT
    That bit you said to the guy in London. That you were going to fix up the old plays. For your legacy.

PLAYWRIGHT
    I certainly did not use the term "fix."

ASSISTANT
    Or whatever.

PLAYWRIGHT
    "Revisit them," I said.

ASSISTANT
    All right, well, whatever then.

PLAYWRIGHT
    Why, do you feel they need fixing?

ASSISTANT
It was you who said it.

PLAYWRIGHT
I said "revisit."

ASSISTANT
Oh, fine.

PLAYWRIGHT
I am taught in universities I think you may have forgotten.

ASSISTANT
Yes, yes, they're all perfect.

PLAYWRIGHT
Why, what would you fix?

ASSISTANT
Oh, forget it, I was just being nice.

PLAYWRIGHT
Nice? As if you were capable of it.

ASSISTANT
Oh, yes, I'm a monster.

PLAYWRIGHT
What would you fix?

ASSISTANT
I don't know.

PLAYWRIGHT
Come on now, fifteen years with me, you must have a thought in your head. What would you fix?

ASSISTANT
A few more happy endings maybe.

PLAYWRIGHT
(*laughing*) Happy endings? Happy endings are an evil fiction.

ASSISTANT
There's no such thing as a happy ending?

PLAYWRIGHT
Poetry is much more sophisticated than that.

ASSISTANT
> Is that what you think you are, sophisticated? This life is
> sophisticated? Misery's sophisticated?

PLAYWRIGHT
> "Misery"? I'd hardly call our lives misery.

ASSISTANT
> Well what would you call it?

PLAYWRIGHT
> I thought we were having fun.

ASSISTANT
> You're not serious.

> *A moment.*

PLAYWRIGHT
> (*a private joke*) You owe me twenty dollars.

ASSISTANT
> (*lightening up*) Oh, shut up.

> *The PLAYWRIGHT chuckles to himself.*

> Let's get a move on.

PLAYWRIGHT
> No more interviews.

ASSISTANT
> I know.

PLAYWRIGHT
> Not today.

ASSISTANT
> I know.

PLAYWRIGHT
> Today is opening day. Tonight is opening night.

ASSISTANT
> I know.

PLAYWRIGHT
> Speaking of which, will I have an escort for this evening?

ASSISTANT
Yes, me.

PLAYWRIGHT
No no, that wouldn't look right, me coming in there in the personal company of someone in my own employ.

ASSISTANT
What's the difference, you'll be employing the escort.

PLAYWRIGHT
No no, it's all about appearances, now we've got to keep up the appearances. This is a very special night, I need a little something special.

ASSISTANT
We'll see.

PLAYWRIGHT
You could get yourself an escort for this evening as well.

ASSISTANT
Forget it.

PLAYWRIGHT
Why not?

ASSISTANT
Not in the mood.

PLAYWRIGHT
You're more and more like an old lady in a nursing home.

ASSISTANT
And you're like a little boy in a candy store.

PLAYWRIGHT
Well I am. And it is.

ASSISTANT
Yeah well candy gives you metabolic arthritis.

PLAYWRIGHT
Oh, Daddy, can't I have some candy?

ASSISTANT
Oh, shut up.

PLAYWRIGHT
Well there's no reason I shouldn't have a little fun, just tonight.

ASSISTANT
No more "just tonights."

PLAYWRIGHT
Oh, please.

ASSISTANT
Stop it.

PLAYWRIGHT
Please, Daddy, please may I have a pony.

ASSISTANT
(laughing) Shut up.

PLAYWRIGHT
A pretty little pony. Please?

ASSISTANT
Well I do have a surprise for you.

PLAYWRIGHT
(clapping his hands together gleefully) A surprise!

ASSISTANT
The theatre agreed to put out for a tux for you for tonight.

PLAYWRIGHT
I'll be wearing my white linen tonight.

ASSISTANT
You messed that up in London, that's no good now.

PLAYWRIGHT
Oh, yes, the white linen was a casualty of that ordeal wasn't it.

ASSISTANT
They'll take you down this afternoon and fit you.

PLAYWRIGHT
A tuxedo. That would be festive. Properly celebratory.

ASSISTANT
You like that?

PLAYWRIGHT
Yes, that would be suitable.

ASSISTANT
(sarcastic) You're welcome.

PLAYWRIGHT
Thank you. You're so "nice."

ASSISTANT
Oh, shut up.

The ASSISTANT crosses to the PLAYWRIGHT.

PLAYWRIGHT
We'll have a lovely time then. Won't we? Let's. Just tonight, a lovely time. Some fun?

The ASSISTANT takes the PLAYWRIGHT's drink.

ASSISTANT
Go get yourself cleaned up.

The PLAYWRIGHT heads toward the bathroom.

PLAYWRIGHT
I'll be but a moment.

The PLAYWRIGHT steps into the bathroom and sees himself in a mirror there.

Or an hour.

The PLAYWRIGHT turns back a moment.

And if you can't find a pony, a young Warren Beatty will do.

The PLAYWRIGHT closes the door.

ASSISTANT
Christ.

Left alone, the ASSISTANT knocks the PLAYWRIGHT's drink back in one. Blackout.

SCENE TWO   Thursday Evening

The YOUNG MAN is seated. He is twenty-eight, a life lived, but still youthful. He rises and walks around the room, inspecting it. He looks out the window. He picks up a slim book on the bedside table. He looks at it a moment. He puts it back. He looks toward the door. He opens a drawer in the bedside table. He picks up the Bible that lives there. He flips through it, he drops it back in the drawer. He closes the drawer. He takes a cigarette from his pocket and lights a lighter.

ASSISTANT
(*entering*) No smoking.

The ASSISTANT enters wearing a leather jacket over his dress shirt and pants, he cuts a darker figure than we have seen before. He carries a garment bag, he hangs it up and takes from it a formal shirt, pants and two jackets.

YOUNG MAN
What?

ASSISTANT
No smoking. If you smoke, he'll smoke, and he's not smoking.

YOUNG MAN
No smoking?

ASSISTANT
Not in the room.

YOUNG MAN
What the fuck am I supposed to do, hang out the window?

ASSISTANT
And watch your language, he doesn't like it.

YOUNG MAN
Are you one of those born-agains or something?

ASSISTANT
Yeah, I brought you up here to save your soul.

YOUNG MAN
You serious?

ASSISTANT
Well, we've established that you have no sense of humour.

YOUNG MAN
It happens, man. I mean, you've got the Bible there.

ASSISTANT
Where?

YOUNG MAN
In the drawer there.

ASSISTANT
What were you doing in the drawer?

YOUNG MAN
Checking for my safety, right. I don't know, you might be some freak, butcher knives in the drawers, rope under the bed.

ASSISTANT
It's a hotel room, they all come with Bibles, sweetheart. Have you not done this before?

YOUNG MAN
I been in lots of hotel rooms, no Bible.

ASSISTANT
This a bit upscale for you?

YOUNG MAN
The world's full of freaks, man.

ASSISTANT
It is, isn't it.

YOUNG MAN
So where's your friend?

ASSISTANT
On his way. Are you clean?

YOUNG MAN
Yeah I'm clean. You want to taste me and find out?

ASSISTANT
Drugs. I mean drugs.

YOUNG MAN
You want drugs?

ASSISTANT
No drugs. You hear me? No drugs.

YOUNG MAN
You friend doesn't like drugs?

ASSISTANT
They don't like him.

YOUNG MAN
Yeah, yeah, your "friend." I don't see no friend.

The YOUNG MAN approaches the ASSISTANT.

Is your friend made up? Is that the deal? You one of those guys pretends it's not for you? We can say it's your friend. That's all right by me. You want to meet my friend?

The ASSISTANT ignores him. He throws the pants and shirt on the bed.

ASSISTANT
Put that on. It's mine, don't mess it up. You've been to a play before?

YOUNG MAN
Yeah. What do you mean a "play"?

ASSISTANT
The theatre, a play.

YOUNG MAN
I don't know. Yeah. One time or something. What kind of play?

ASSISTANT
"A dark and haunting vision of civilization on the brink of destruction."

YOUNG MAN
They got a bar there?

ASSISTANT
(indicates the whiskey) You can have a drink here if you want. Pace yourself. Don't get messy.

The YOUNG MAN heads for the bottle.

Put that on first.

The YOUNG MAN begins to change in a showy fashion. The ASSISTANT pays him little attention as he puts on a formal jacket.

You'll go to the play. Don't say anything about it unless he asks, and if he does ask say it was brilliant. Try it. Say, "It was brilliant."

YOUNG MAN
(badly) "It was brilliant."

ASSISTANT
I guess if he's drunk enough he'd believe it. You'll go to the party with him, don't go wandering off. I'll be there keeping an eye on you. He'll get drunk, you'll come back here, let him do all the talking, he'll get drunker and pass out. You should be out of here by midnight.

YOUNG MAN
Midnight? That's my whole night. That's going to cost you.

ASSISTANT
We settled on a hundred.

YOUNG MAN
A hundred and twenty.

ASSISTANT
Fine.

> The YOUNG MAN poses for the ASSISTANT.

YOUNG MAN
What do you think?

ASSISTANT
You'll do. Put that on.

> The YOUNG MAN continues to change in a perfunctory fashion.

How old are you?

YOUNG MAN
Twenty-one.

ASSISTANT
(laughing) At one time maybe.

YOUNG MAN
Are you calling me a liar?

ASSISTANT
Show me some ID.

YOUNG MAN
Get outta here.

ASSISTANT
Show me some ID or the deal's off.

YOUNG MAN
Twenty-four.

ASSISTANT
ID now.

> *The YOUNG MAN takes his wallet from his pants. He throws a driver's licence at the ASSISTANT. The ASSISTANT picks it up. The YOUNG MAN continues dressing.*

(*checking the licence*) Twenty-eight. That's closer to the truth I guess.

YOUNG MAN
I get carded all the time, man, I pass for eighteen.

ASSISTANT
To the blind maybe.

YOUNG MAN
Are you going stop insulting me or am I going to leave?

ASSISTANT
Buck up, junior. You better; if you think I'm bad, he's worse.

> *The ASSISTANT looks at the licence again.*

Nova Scotia? You're far from home.

YOUNG MAN
I got a lot of homes, man.

> *The ASSISTANT hands the ID back to the YOUNG MAN. The ASSISTANT takes a tie out of a drawer, he holds it out for the YOUNG MAN.*

What's that, a blindfold?

> *The ASSISTANT tosses the tie at the YOUNG MAN.*

ASSISTANT
You've never seen a tie before? Put it on.

YOUNG MAN
Why do I got to wear a tie for?

ASSISTANT
It's a premiere. An opening. It's his play.

YOUNG MAN
Who?

ASSISTANT
My friend.

YOUNG MAN
His play how?

ASSISTANT
He wrote it. He's written a lot. *(indicating the book on the bedside table)* That's one of his right there.

The YOUNG MAN looks at the book.

YOUNG MAN
Yeah, I saw that. That's his name?

ASSISTANT
Yes.

YOUNG MAN
That his real name?

ASSISTANT
Real enough.

YOUNG MAN
I never heard of him.

ASSISTANT
Don't tell him that.

The ASSISTANT takes a tie from the pocket of his jacket and puts it on. The YOUNG MAN stands in the mirror struggling with his tie.

YOUNG MAN
I seen a play before. People talking all English-like. Like James Bond but old times. Everybody died at the end.

ASSISTANT
That would be called a tragedy.

YOUNG MAN
Does everybody die in this one?

ASSISTANT

No. People don't usually die at the end of his. Which I guess that's the tragedy of his plays. People have to keep on living.

YOUNG MAN

It's all fake anyway, man.

ASSISTANT

Isn't it.

The YOUNG MAN continues to struggle with the tie.

You don't know how to tie a tie?

YOUNG MAN

This one's weird or something.

ASSISTANT

Come here.

The ASSISTANT begins to tie the YOUNG MAN's tie for him.

I've passed through Nova Scotia before. What part are you from?

YOUNG MAN

You wouldn't notice it if you passed through it. You wouldn't notice it if you lived there for sixteen years.

ASSISTANT

Try me.

YOUNG MAN

The place between the place with a steel mill that doesn't make steel and the place with the coal mine that's got no coal.

ASSISTANT

So what brings you all the way to Vancouver?

YOUNG MAN

I'm just passing through, man. I'm on my way to LA. I'm getting into the movies.

ASSISTANT

Fame and fortune.

YOUNG MAN

Why not.

ASSISTANT
A young Warren Beatty.

YOUNG MAN
Oh, yeah, he's cool, "Bonnie and Clyde," fuckin' good movie. But not that kind of movie, no. I met this guy a couple months ago, up here from LA, he makes adult films. You know, pornos? And I'm good at sex, see, I've got lots of stamina. Plus I've got a specialized talent, I'm what they call an aggressive bottom.

ASSISTANT
How nice for you.

YOUNG MAN
What are you? Or do you like just to watch?

ASSISTANT
Los Angeles can be a little rough.

YOUNG MAN
That's okay, I can be a little rough.

The YOUNG MAN presses his pelvis into the ASSISTANT.

The ASSISTANT moves away.

ASSISTANT
Your tie's done.

YOUNG MAN
Thanks.

ASSISTANT
Can you read?

YOUNG MAN
Can I read? Yeah, I can read, what do you think, I'm retarded?

The ASSISTANT holds out the jacket for the YOUNG MAN. The YOUNG MAN steps into the jacket.

ASSISTANT
He might to ask you to read. It's part of what he does. He'll ask you to read for him. Probably from the Bible. He's not some born-again though, just the Bible's always handy.

YOUNG MAN
He wants me to read the Bible? That's weird, man.

ASSISTANT
There's no end to the insanity.

YOUNG MAN
Whatever gets you off, I guess.

ASSISTANT
It's not about me.

The YOUNG MAN approaches the ASSISTANT. He comes close.

YOUNG MAN
What if it was? What would you want?

ASSISTANT
Just keep him entertained.

YOUNG MAN
Why did you pick me?

ASSISTANT
I know his type.

YOUNG MAN
What about later?

ASSISTANT
What about later?

YOUNG MAN
You got a room too?

ASSISTANT
I've got a room.

YOUNG MAN
I'd like to see your room.

Noise off. The PLAYWRIGHT has returned.

ASSISTANT
Sit. Speak when spoken to.

The YOUNG MAN sits. The ASSISTANT steps to the door to greet the PLAYWRIGHT.

The PLAYWRIGHT enters, pushing past the ASSISTANT. He is handsome in his tuxedo, but a terrible mess of nerves. The PLAYWRIGHT does not see the YOUNG MAN.

PLAYWRIGHT

Oh, I can't, I just can't, I can't do it.

ASSISTANT

What are you talking about?

The PLAYWRIGHT goes to the table and pours a drink.

PLAYWRIGHT

I'm a wreck, I'm just a wreck. It's going to be a disaster, I just know it. I could barely make it back here. Oh, please, I can't go.

ASSISTANT

Stop that. Look at you, you're walking around not limping or anything.

PLAYWRIGHT

Because I can't feel my legs. I can't feel anything. I'm all trussed up like a Thanksgiving turkey. Call them, tell them anything, let's just leave, let's fly home, I can't do it.

ASSISTANT

No.

The PLAYWRIGHT collapses onto the bed, near tears.

PLAYWRIGHT

Oh, please, oh, please don't make me. I can't face it, really I can't. The hounds, the wolves. Please don't make me go. I haven't got it in me, I have nothing left, really I don't.

ASSISTANT

You um?

The PLAYWRIGHT looks up.

(indicating the YOUNG MAN) You have a guest.

The PLAYWRIGHT looks over and sees the YOUNG MAN. His demeanour turns on a dime.

PLAYWRIGHT

Oh, I see. Well.

The PLAYWRIGHT rises and regards the YOUNG MAN.

Well. Well well well well well well. He's very nice.

(to the ASSISTANT) You *do* care. Get me a little drink would you, just an inch.

ASSISTANT

Half an inch. We have to go.

> *The ASSISTANT pours a small drink and hands it to the PLAYWRIGHT.*

PLAYWRIGHT

(to the ASSISTANT, about the YOUNG MAN) He's very nice. And he comes in a suit.

ASSISTANT

It's mine, and make sure he doesn't mess it up.

PLAYWRIGHT

(to the ASSISTANT) Very nice. Does he talk?

YOUNG MAN

Yeah. And he reads, too.

PLAYWRIGHT

What? Oh, you're telling him stories are you?

ASSISTANT

I'm preparing him.

PLAYWRIGHT

Oh, I don't do that anymore. That was just a childish diversion. Now I'm simply interested in the handsome company of a fine young man.

(to the ASSISTANT) Is there one for you as well?

ASSISTANT

I'm fine, thanks.

YOUNG MAN

There's lots of me to go around.

PLAYWRIGHT

(laughing) I bet there is.

(to the ASSISTANT) You hear that, my my, but unfortunately you don't like to share anymore, do you?

ASSISTANT

No. Come on, we have to go.

PLAYWRIGHT

(to the YOUNG MAN) This, you've certainly deduced, is my trusted and loyal assistant of many years. Surely you've made close acquaintance.

YOUNG MAN

He's shy.

PLAYWRIGHT

"He's shy"! Oh, my, yes, shy like a switchblade.

YOUNG MAN

What?

PLAYWRIGHT

Oh, no, I jest. He's as harmless as a litter of kittens.

(to the ASSISTANT) But since you two have gotten to know one another, give me a moment or two alone with my young friend and I'll be along presently.

ASSISTANT

We have to go.

PLAYWRIGHT

We'll meet you in the lobby. Get us a car. Two or three minutes.

ASSISTANT

Two minutes.

PLAYWRIGHT

Yes, yes, give or take thirty seconds.

The ASSISTANT moves to leave. He stops, he picks up the bottle and heads out with it.

Where are you going with that?

ASSISTANT

I'll leave it at the desk, we'll pick it up on our way back in.

PLAYWRIGHT

So untrusting.

The ASSISTANT leaves.

ASSISTANT

(off) Two minutes!

*The PLAYWRIGHT regards the YOUNG MAN. The YOUNG
MAN sits, assured, cocky, feeling his power.*

PLAYWRIGHT
I must apologize for my nervous state when I first entered. It is
a very important night for me, I'm just a little wound up.

YOUNG MAN
No sweat.

PLAYWRIGHT
How old are you? Twenty? Twenty-one?

YOUNG MAN
Twenty.

PLAYWRIGHT
Yes. Not even yet in your prime.

YOUNG MAN
Oh, I'm prime, I'm as prime as they get.

PLAYWRIGHT
Do you know who I am?

YOUNG MAN
Yeah. That's your book. You're famous.

PLAYWRIGHT
Well, I have been celebrated in certain circles, yes.

YOUNG MAN
Yeah, me too.

PLAYWRIGHT
I'm sure. But what I'm wondering is, if a young man such as yourself
might have the wherewithal to acquire perhaps, something that
might help stimulate my vaguely fatigued spirit.

YOUNG MAN
Oh, I can be very stimulating.

PLAYWRIGHT
Yes, no doubt. But I was thinking perhaps in another form.

YOUNG MAN
Like what?

PLAYWRIGHT

In a powdered form perhaps?

YOUNG MAN

Your buddy said no drugs.

PLAYWRIGHT

Ah, yes, His Greatness does like to present me as being troubled in that area but really, that's his issue. I try to deal with my own concerns. So as not to tempt him from the sober path he has chosen to trod. If you follow me?

YOUNG MAN

Yeah, I follow you. I know some people.

PLAYWRIGHT

Wonderful, wonderful. And now what shall we call you?

YOUNG MAN

I'm—

PLAYWRIGHT

No no no. Let's just call you the Young Gentleman.

YOUNG MAN

I don't how much of a gentleman I'll be.

PLAYWRIGHT

For now. We'll drop the gentleman later.

YOUNG MAN

You can drop me, bend me over, whatever you want.

PLAYWRIGHT

Well, well. Come then, let's to church.

YOUNG MAN

I thought we were going to a play.

PLAYWRIGHT

Oh, yes, but the theatre is my church. Art is my God. Come along then. I think it's going to be a wonderful evening.

YOUNG MAN

I think it's going to be brilliant.

PLAYWRIGHT

Yes indeed, indeed it may be. Come along, our carriage awaits.

The PLAYWRIGHT ushers the YOUNG MAN out.

(exiting) Come along then.

Blackout.

SCENE THREE   Thursday Night

Noises off as the three enter, back from the opening night party. Spirits are high, great drunken bonhomie.

They enter in the dark, the ASSISTANT and the YOUNG MAN are bubbling with excitement, the PLAYWRIGHT is beaming, calmly in control, vindicated. They are all a little drunk.

ASSISTANT
Amazing! Amazing!

YOUNG MAN
And they all stood up and clapped at the end.

ASSISTANT
At the end, even at the beginning. They gave him an ovation when he walked in.

YOUNG MAN
The end was excellent.

ASSISTANT
They got it, they really got it.

> *The ASSISTANT turns on the lights. He carries a few bottles brought home from the party.*

I even got it. I don't think I did before, but this time it all made sense.

YOUNG MAN
It was brilliant. It really was.

ASSISTANT
(to the PLAYWRIGHT) And you were good. You didn't insult anyone.

PLAYWRIGHT
Well who would I insult? It was impeccably executed. Impeccably.

ASSISTANT

And you know? In the theatre tonight, it reminded me what it's
all about. It's all about believing in the moment. Letting go of
everything else. And for that moment it's like everything's right
with the world, even if it's a tragedy. Because it's not about whether
it's tragic or happy or bad or good or whatever, it's just all about the
believing. And they were, everybody was believing. The audience, the
actors. And the actors weren't half bad.

PLAYWRIGHT

Oh, don't be stingy now, they were wonderful. The tall girl was a bit
of a horseface unfortunately. But it added to the pathos don't you
think?

ASSISTANT

Oh, she was great.

YOUNG MAN

The big one, yeah, she was good.

ASSISTANT

· She was great.

> *The ASSISTANT pours drinks all round.*

PLAYWRIGHT

(to the YOUNG MAN) So you liked it?

YOUNG MAN

It was brilliant.

PLAYWRIGHT

You think so?

YOUNG MAN

I mean, first it all seemed a bit kind of fake, but then I really got into
it. I, like, really believed them and everything.

PLAYWRIGHT

Well "believing them and everything" is what it's all about.

ASSISTANT

Yes, yes, exactly.

YOUNG MAN

And no, but, like, and at the end, and everybody's all freaking out
and that guy's howling and they're all jumping off the stage. It was

amazing. And people were like all watching it like: *(makes a face of jaw-dropped amazement)* They were, I looked at them, they were like: *(makes a face of jaw-dropped amazement)*

PLAYWRIGHT

(to the YOUNG MAN) You were shaking.

(to the ASSISTANT) He was shaking.

(to the YOUNG MAN) At one point you were shaking like a leaf.

YOUNG MAN

Yeah I was. When that guy came at the other guy. I was like, shaking, man. I was like going to jump up there and get into it with them.

PLAYWRIGHT

I know, I know.

YOUNG MAN

I was loving it. I mean it was really brilliant. And I'm not just saying that because he told me to.

PLAYWRIGHT

(to the ASSISTANT) You told him to say it was brilliant?

ASSISTANT

I didn't know what he was going to think.

PLAYWRIGHT

(to the ASSISTANT) Aren't you nice.

ASSISTANT

It was brilliant.

YOUNG MAN

It really, really was. I mean, I saw a play before.

PLAYWRIGHT

You did?

ASSISTANT

Shakespeare apparently.

YOUNG MAN

But this was way better.

PLAYWRIGHT

I have heard that comparison in my favour before, I must say.

YOUNG MAN
I was loving it.

The YOUNG MAN pulls a small plastic bag of cocaine from his pocket and shows it to the PLAYWRIGHT.

PLAYWRIGHT
(to the YOUNG MAN) I could feel you loving it.

The PLAYWRIGHT takes the plastic bag from the YOUNG MAN. The ASSISTANT does not see this exchange.

(to the ASSISTANT, about the YOUNG MAN) I think you may have found me a little muse here.

The PLAYWRIGHT heads into the bathroom.

I'm just going to freshen up a bit.

The PLAYWRIGHT closes the door. The ASSISTANT finishes his drink and pours himself another.

YOUNG MAN
That was great. And he wrote it. Wow. The end was sad though. Not bad sad, but sad.

The ASSISTANT approaches the YOUNG MAN.

ASSISTANT
You're a little softie, aren't you.

The ASSISTANT gets close to the YOUNG MAN.

YOUNG MAN
I like him. And he's funny, too. I can see why he's famous. You can tell, just by the way people are to him. And he's got this thing around him.

ASSISTANT
Like an odor?

YOUNG MAN
I even think, like, I could maybe even do that.

ASSISTANT
Do what?

YOUNG MAN
Up on the stage like that, act like that.

ASSISTANT

I bet you could.

YOUNG MAN

It was brilliant.

ASSISTANT

What would you think about seeing my room? A couple of drinks here, do your business with him, make your apologies, somewhere else to be.

YOUNG MAN

With you?

ASSISTANT

A lot more fun than him. What do you say?

YOUNG MAN

I thought I wasn't for you?

ASSISTANT

You're perfect for me.

YOUNG MAN

You're not my type. I don't go for faggy guys. No offence.

The PLAYWRIGHT re-enters. He picks up the bottle and pours a drink for himself and the YOUNG MAN.

PLAYWRIGHT

I know what we need to do now. Let's revel in the accolades.

(to the ASSISTANT) You go out and get the papers, let's see how they've responded to our triumphant evening.

ASSISTANT

The papers won't be out till morning.

PLAYWRIGHT

Well we'll wait up till morning.

ASSISTANT

Let's not push it. You've had a night of it already.

YOUNG MAN

Will there be stuff in the paper?

PLAYWRIGHT

"Stuff," yes there will be "stuff." And there was a time when I would have been fearful of that "stuff," the snakes in the grass, the sharks following a trace of blood in the water, but now, tonight, today, I have no fear. The snakes but snails, the sharks, minnows. The tide has turned.

YOUNG MAN
(to the PLAYWRIGHT) Everybody was, like: (jaw-dropped amazement) I saw them. I was, too.

PLAYWRIGHT
It's been a while since I've said this, but I am feeling inspired. I feel, still I do feel compelled to revisit the old plays with a keener eye, a sharper sense of my message, but as well I'm feeling something else. A new play I think.

YOUNG MAN
Cool.

PLAYWRIGHT
Something is brewing, I feel, something dangerous.

YOUNG MAN
(to the PLAYWRIGHT) Oh, yeah, man, you're amazing. I mean, if I could, I would totally be in a play of yours, I mean if I could, I don't know.

PLAYWRIGHT
It requires a certain spirit. And you are a very spirited young man.

ASSISTANT
(to the PLAYWRIGHT) How's your gout, do you need to sit down?

PLAYWRIGHT
I'm fine. Practically floating.

ASSISTANT
The critics were out in full force.

PLAYWRIGHT
And there couldn't have been a better night for them. The room was with us.

ASSISTANT
Don't set yourself up for a fall. Remember what happened in London.

PLAYWRIGHT
Oh, no, no, they were all on side, they were all on side tonight.

ASSISTANT
The girl from the radio interview was there.

PLAYWRIGHT
Judy wasn't it?

ASSISTANT
Julie. The one you hung up on.

PLAYWRIGHT
Well Julie has seen now, hasn't she. The room was electric, my audience has come on side once again.

ASSISTANT
Apparently she's doing a review on the radio tomorrow night. I doubt it was "modern" enough for her.

> *The PLAYWRIGHT regards the ASSISTANT a moment.*

PLAYWRIGHT
(to the YOUNG MAN) Why don't you freshen up while I have a word with my friend.

> *The YOUNG MAN steps into the bathroom. The PLAYWRIGHT closes the door. He speaks in a private, hushed tone.*

Why are you doing this?

ASSISTANT
I'm not doing anything. You know how it goes.

PLAYWRIGHT
Well I know how it has gone, and I know I no longer want to go there, nor do I want to be dragged there. I think you should go.

ASSISTANT
No.

PLAYWRIGHT
I say go to your room. Go on. I want to have a moment with my young man.

ASSISTANT
Yeah, well, you should have seen your young man coming on to me before.

PLAYWRIGHT

You stop it now. Stop it. Look at yourself. Look how you get. Pinched and spiteful.

ASSISTANT

Do I?

PLAYWRIGHT

Yes. Why is that?

ASSISTANT

Years with you, I guess.

PLAYWRIGHT

You call it misery. That's your name. Don't you drag me down into your misery.

ASSISTANT

You are my misery.

PLAYWRIGHT

Well then leave your misery and go to your room.

ASSISTANT

He hasn't been paid.

PLAYWRIGHT

I'll take care of that.

ASSISTANT

Where did you get money?

PLAYWRIGHT

You are not my keeper.

ASSISTANT

I'm not?

PLAYWRIGHT

You are not my wife.

ASSISTANT

Well what the hell am I then? Tell me that? How do you think this makes me feel?

PLAYWRIGHT

Your feelings are your own concern. This is my night.

ASSISTANT

(*loudly*) It's always your night. What about me?

PLAYWRIGHT

Keep your voice down. God Almighty, when did you get to be such a pitiful drunk?

The ASSISTANT takes a moment, realizes he is quite drunk.

Don't embarrass yourself. Go on now. Go.

A moment. Without a word the ASSISTANT leaves.

The PLAYWRIGHT quickly moves about the room, limping slightly. He pours himself a drink. He turns down the lights, only the bedside lamp left on, blue light from the parking lot outside through the window. He adjusts himself on the bed comfortably. He turns on the radio on the bedside table and moves through stations until he finds something suitable, Beethoven's "Pathétique."

The YOUNG MAN re-enters. He stands with the blue light behind him. He regards the PLAYWRIGHT.

YOUNG MAN

He's gone, is he?

PLAYWRIGHT

He is gone.

YOUNG MAN

Is he your boyfriend?

PLAYWRIGHT

He's more my jailer. If there's a difference.

YOUNG MAN

But you're the boss.

PLAYWRIGHT

I am.

YOUNG MAN

You want to do a line?

PLAYWRIGHT

I just did, my dear. I'm fine, I'm fine.

YOUNG MAN

I like you.

PLAYWRIGHT

Why don't you take off your clothes now.

Silently the YOUNG MAN undresses. The PLAYWRIGHT watches him, his every move. The YOUNG MAN gets down to his underwear. The PLAYWRIGHT stops him.

Leave that. As you are.

The YOUNG MAN moves to approach the PLAYWRIGHT. The PLAYWRIGHT stops him.

No, there. As you are. You're beautiful.

YOUNG MAN

I can read. Do you want me to read to you?

PLAYWRIGHT

I would like that, yes.

YOUNG MAN

Do you want me to read the Bible?

PLAYWRIGHT

No. Here.

The PLAYWRIGHT hands the YOUNG MAN the book from the bedside table.

It's a special night. Read one of mine.

The YOUNG MAN takes the book.

You are beautiful. You are perfect. You are an angel.

The YOUNG MAN opens the book to read as the lights fade.

End of ACT ONE.

ACT TWO

SCENE ONE   Friday Morning

The ASSISTANT enters the darkened hotel room with newspapers under his arm. A lamp is on. He places the newspapers on the desk. He crosses to the window and opens the curtains. The grey light of a rainy day enters the room.

ASSISTANT
A perfect day for rain.

The ASSISTANT turns and is startled to see the PLAYWRIGHT sitting in a chair, his back turned to the ASSISTANT, his elbows on his knees, his head in his hands.

Christ! Oh. You almost gave me a heart attack. I thought you'd still be dead to the world.

The PLAYWRIGHT does not react.

I've got a head on me like it was New Year's Day.

The ASSISTANT goes to the desk and picks up the papers. He considers showing the PLAYWRIGHT the reviews but then thinks better of it. The ASSISTANT wanders into the bathroom.

(off) And I guess you're not much better. It was the champagne at the theatre that did it. Never mix, never worry, right? I meant to take a Tylenol before I went to bed but I just passed out. That cocky little bastard, he was something, wasn't he. We're well rid of him. Reminded me of that one in Chicago. Not as smart but the same attitude.

The ASSISTANT comes back into the room.

How did that all end up?

The ASSISTANT moves to the bed. He notices it's been made. He looks around the room. It's been cleaned.

Has the maid been in? Did you let the maid in? Has the maid been in?

PLAYWRIGHT
It appears so, yes.

ASSISTANT

You let the maid in?

The ASSISTANT notices the PLAYWRIGHT is fully dressed, and also wet, from having been outside.

What are you doing dressed? And all wet, look at you. You've been out?

PLAYWRIGHT

I've been out.

The ASSISTANT brings the PLAYWRIGHT a towel from the bathroom.

ASSISTANT

Where did you go? You've been out? It's not even noon and you're up and out? You've been out?

PLAYWRIGHT

Leave me! I said I've been out, shut up already.

The ASSISTANT takes a moment, he realizes the PLAYWRIGHT has probably seen the reviews.

ASSISTANT

Oh, I see. I see I see I see.

The ASSISTANT goes to the desk and picks up the papers.

Yes. You've been out then, all right. I see.

PLAYWRIGHT

I have been out.

ASSISTANT

Yes. It's not so good is it.

PLAYWRIGHT

It's been worse.

ASSISTANT

Yes, not much, but yes. London was almost as bad.

PLAYWRIGHT

Rained every damn day in London.

ASSISTANT

And that, too.

*The ASSISTANT drops the papers in the wastepaper basket near
the desk. The ASSISTANT is quiet a moment. He wanders about
the room not sure what to do. He watches the PLAYWRIGHT,
feeling sympathy. He sits on the bed.*

Well, you know. What the hell. Who cares, right? Really? What does
it matter in the end?

*The ASSISTANT looks to the PLAYWRIGHT for a response. There
is none.*

You want a cup of tea?

The PLAYWRIGHT shakes his head no.

I don't know how you do it, how you put yourself out there, how
you have to take it. From people who— Well who are they, what
have they ever done? Find fault, judge, complain—as if they could
do better right? I give you a hard time but—I couldn't do it. Well
I tried and I couldn't.

The ASSISTANT rises and approaches the PLAYWRIGHT.

Look at you all soaking wet. What were you doing out wandering
around in the rain, forget about all them. Whatever we are we've got
us I guess.

A moment.

How about a hot bath? Would you like that?

*Noise off. The ASSISTANT steps toward the door, the
PLAYWRIGHT looks up expectantly.*

*The YOUNG MAN enters, wet from the rain, he carries a small
paper bag from a drug store and a bag from the liquor store
containing beer and a large bottle of whiskey. He places the liquor
on the desk and drops the room keys there. The ASSISTANT
watches him, slightly agog.*

YOUNG MAN
Shit, man, this rain? Good you came back when you did. It's pissing
now. I thought we were gonna be good for a while. Last two days,
right, last two days were great, but now that it's back? Like this could
go on for a month even. At least. Weather sucks here, man.
Summer's nice though.

(to the ASSISTANT) Hi.

The YOUNG MAN hands the PLAYWRIGHT the small paper bag. The PLAYWRIGHT rises and heads for the bathroom.

ASSISTANT
(regarding the bag) What the hell is that?

PLAYWRIGHT
Something for my headache, which has been pounding on the back of my eyeballs for the better part of the last half hour.

ASSISTANT
The booze is for your headache, too, is it?

PLAYWRIGHT
It'll probably end up doing a far sight better for it than you have, babbling away at me. You've done nothing but exacerbate it.

(to the YOUNG MAN) Thank you.

YOUNG MAN
No sweat.

The PLAYWRIGHT enters the bathroom.

The ASSISTANT regards the YOUNG MAN. The YOUNG MAN opens a beer. He offers one to the ASSISTANT.

ASSISTANT
I don't think so.

YOUNG MAN
(continuing to hold out the beer) My take is, after hanging out with him for a while, it seems like either you're going to wanna join the party or you're gonna wanna go.

The ASSISTANT takes the beer from the YOUNG MAN and puts it back on the desk with the others.

ASSISTANT
I know your game.

YOUNG MAN
What's my game?

ASSISTANT
You can't con him because you've got to go through me to get to him.

YOUNG MAN

And you can't con a con? Is that what you're saying?

ASSISTANT

You think this is the first time this happened? It's not the first time all right, trust me. You'll be paid the hundred and twenty we agreed on.

YOUNG MAN

I won't be paid anything.

ASSISTANT

Then you're free to go.

YOUNG MAN

I mean at least not till the end of the month. I'll just get my cheque when you get yours.

ASSISTANT

What?

YOUNG MAN

I'm on staff, man.

ASSISTANT

Staff?

YOUNG MAN

I'm part of the family now.

ASSISTANT

Oh, no, he's up to that again, is he? God, if I had a dime for every time he'd got up to that, I'd be able to pay your hourly rate a few times over.

YOUNG MAN

So who's the boss, you?

ASSISTANT

Listen, there's no staff. There's me and there's him and that's it. And? I mean, he may have been up for a bit of it last night, but that's very rare these days.

YOUNG MAN

Oh yeah, he was doing all right last night.

ASSISTANT

Well that's an exception. But what I mean is, there's no call for your services on a regular basis.

YOUNG MAN

No no no, see, no what we've got going in that way, that's personal. The other thing is, the real thing is, is a business thing.

ASSISTANT

What business?

YOUNG MAN

He's got jobs for me.

ASSISTANT

Like?

YOUNG MAN

He's going to write something for me.

ASSISTANT

What?

YOUNG MAN

This new thing he's going to write for me to be an actor in.

ASSISTANT

What thing?

YOUNG MAN

It's going to be a machine for me.

ASSISTANT

A machine? What do you mean?

YOUNG MAN

For me. A machine or whatever. A thing, a... like a car? Not like a car but you call it that.

ASSISTANT

Sorry?

YOUNG MAN

Like a car— A machine. For me like?

ASSISTANT

A vehicle?

YOUNG MAN
Yeah yeah yeah, a vehicle for me.

ASSISTANT
You do understand that's not going to happen.

YOUNG MAN
We'll see.

ASSISTANT
I think you'd be better off taking your hundred and twenty now and cutting your losses.

The PLAYWRIGHT comes out of the bathroom. He gets himself a drink.

PLAYWRIGHT
There now, a little clean up and a couple of pills for my head, and I'm already feeling better.

YOUNG MAN
(to the PLAYWRIGHT) What's that other thing I am?

PLAYWRIGHT
You, my dear, are gorgeous.

YOUNG MAN
No, that thing I'm going to be. The angel, like, of ideas.

PLAYWRIGHT
My muse, yes, my muse. Let's close up these drapes to the vulgar day.

(to the YOUNG MAN) Get some lights on there, would you? Let's give it the feel of evening, early evening. Cocktail hour.

The YOUNG MAN turns the lamps on.

ASSISTANT
No no no, if you start drinking now you'll miss your nap.

PLAYWRIGHT
Napping's for you old ladies. I am slept, I am well slept, I slept the sleep of a satisfied man.

ASSISTANT
No, you'll throw off your schedule.

PLAYWRIGHT
God I'm sick of you telling me what to do. Yip, yip, yip, yip. Didn't
we get rid of that little dog we had. Yip yip yip, shut up.

ASSISTANT
Fine.

PLAYWRIGHT
And now do you think we might enjoy ourselves. Do you think that
might be all right?

ASSISTANT
(quietly; to the PLAYWRIGHT) What's going on?

PLAYWRIGHT
(to the YOUNG MAN) Now what would you call someone like him
up here in Canada? Down home we might say a stick-in-the-mud.
Or in another circle perhaps intransigent. Maybe stubborn. More
descriptive might be unyielding. Oh, how about, perhaps: fuddy-
duddy.

YOUNG MAN
(laughing) Fuddy-duddy, yeah yeah. Or maybe…. We'd say like, we'd
say a tight-ass.

PLAYWRIGHT
Don't know about now, but yes, I suppose at one time he had a tight
ass.

> The YOUNG MAN finds this very funny.

(to the ASSISTANT) Do you suppose you might be able to lighten
up? Just a percentile or two.

> The YOUNG MAN holds out a beer for the ASSISTANT. After
> a moment the ASSISTANT takes the beer from the YOUNG MAN.

ASSISTANT
So you're writing a new play I hear.

PLAYWRIGHT
It's a brilliant idea.

YOUNG MAN
(to the ASSISTANT) Warren Beatty's going to be in it, too.

ASSISTANT
Warren Beatty?

YOUNG MAN
> *(to the ASSISTANT)* He knows him.

ASSISTANT
> Has Warren Beatty ever been in a play?

PLAYWRIGHT
> Or maybe, I'm thinking now, it's a one-man show.

ASSISTANT
> *(indicating the YOUNG MAN)* For this one?

PLAYWRIGHT
> Or we'll see, I don't know. He'll find his place. We all find our place.

ASSISTANT
> Let's see how you feel in a few hours.

PLAYWRIGHT
> Nothing's going to change in a few hours. This isn't last night talking, this is today. Look at him. Don't you just feel it? I look at him and I just want to write. This is what I've been waiting for. I should be writing, that's what I do, like a sailor sails, like a soldier goes into battle, like a chef in his kitchen, like a surgeon with his hand on the failing heart. It is time for me to begin again. It's a wonderful combination of the planets lining up, meeting this beautiful creature, last night's triumph.

ASSISTANT
> Have you not seen the papers?

PLAYWRIGHT
> What papers?

> *A moment.*

> Are the papers out? Where are the papers?

ASSISTANT
> I thought you saw them. You said you were out.

PLAYWRIGHT
> Why didn't you tell me? Idiot. Where are they?

ASSISTANT
> I don't think—

PLAYWRIGHT
Are the papers here?

The YOUNG MAN takes newspapers out of the wastebasket.

YOUNG MAN
Here's papers. Are these the papers?

The ASSISTANT tries to get to the papers first.

ASSISTANT
No, wait, no—

PLAYWRIGHT
Give me those, give me those here.

The PLAYWRIGHT takes the papers from the YOUNG MAN.

ASSISTANT
I don't think you should—

PLAYWRIGHT
Silence, silence, shut up.

The ASSISTANT moves to approach the PLAYWRIGHT.

ASSISTANT
Let me—

PLAYWRIGHT
Leave me!

The PLAYWRIGHT holds out his arm to keep the ASSISTANT away. He stands with his back turned and his arm out as he reads one of the reviews. As he reads, his arm slowly drops. Then his shoulders stoop. Then his head bows slightly. Then finally, the arm holding the paper drops to his side.

Are they all this bad?

ASSISTANT
There's just two.

PLAYWRIGHT
Is the other one this bad?

ASSISTANT
That's the good one.

A moment.

The PLAYWRIGHT throws the paper on the bed, and goes into the bathroom closing the door.

The YOUNG MAN picks up the paper from the bed. He reads. After a moment:

YOUNG MAN
"Fiasco," is that bad?

ASSISTANT
What do you think?

YOUNG MAN
Well, I mean it might be something like festival or... you know.

ASSISTANT
It's bad.

The YOUNG MAN keeps reading. The ASSISTANT goes to the door of the bathroom.

(quietly to the PLAYWRIGHT) Can I come in?

PLAYWRIGHT
(off; yelling) Leave me!

The ASSISTANT moves away from the door.

YOUNG MAN
(pronouncing with a hard "g") "Turgid"?

The YOUNG MAN looks at the ASSISTANT hopefully.

ASSISTANT
Turgid is bad.

The YOUNG MAN reads on.

YOUNG MAN
(mispronouncing) "Dis-sing-en-ous."

ASSISTANT
"Disingenuous." Bad.

The YOUNG MAN reads on.

YOUNG MAN
I mean, I know "embarrassing" is mostly bad but is it even bad in a play? I mean, it should be embarrassing, right, yelling and going nuts and that in front of a bunch of strangers, I mean—

ASSISTANT
No. It's all bad.

YOUNG MAN
But so what, I mean, what does it mean?

ASSISTANT
You should probably go, he's not going to be in very good shape when he comes out of there.

YOUNG MAN
No, but I mean no, like, so they get to put this in the paper, does he get to put something in the paper that says they're full of shit or whatever.

ASSISTANT
That's not how it works.

YOUNG MAN
Well why not, I mean, are they right? So is that right what they said?

ASSISTANT
It's just their opinion.

YOUNG MAN
But why do they get to be right?

> The PLAYWRIGHT steps out of the bathroom. The ASSISTANT and the YOUNG MAN grow quiet in the wake of the PLAYWRIGHT's deep silence. The PLAYWRIGHT walks silently through the room. He stands with his back turned.

ASSISTANT
Have a cup of tea.

> The PLAYWRIGHT doesn't respond.

It's not like we haven't been through this before.

> The ASSISTANT waits to see how the PLAYWRIGHT is reacting to him speaking. The PLAYWRIGHT says nothing.

Just look at this as good. What do you care what they say? It gives you muscle. It's good for the spirit. The fighting spirit. And that's what makes you great. And now you're back out there, in the front lines. Look at this as good, just look at this as all really good.

YOUNG MAN
That's bullshit.

ASSISTANT
Nobody's talking to you.

YOUNG MAN
That's bullshit, man. You should be kicking ass. You should be on the goddamn phone, man, calling those bastards, telling them, you know, what's what.

ASSISTANT
You don't get into all that, you don't stoop to their level.

YOUNG MAN
(to the PLAYWRIGHT) I mean, hey, I know a guy that'll burn down their fucking garage, trash their car, break their hand.

ASSISTANT
That's enough.

YOUNG MAN
Okay, maybe not do it, all right, but at least threaten it.

ASSISTANT
If you'd like to end up in jail.

YOUNG MAN
Or not even threaten it to them, just here, in the room, now, that's the talk you want to talk. They're the bad guys right, they're the bastards. Be talking about making them pay instead of saying, oh, it's okay, lay down and die or whatever.

ASSISTANT
That's not what I'm saying.

YOUNG MAN
I mean, whose side are you on, because I wonder. I mean really. You're all about him you're, like—you're not, like, he's wonderful, he's brilliant, he's amazing, no, you're all acting the boss, you're all, like, he's mean, he's insane, he can't get it up.

ASSISTANT
I did not say—

YOUNG MAN

You did so, "Oh, let's wait until he passes out and then we'll go to my room."

ASSISTANT

You little prick.

YOUNG MAN

(to the PLAYWRIGHT) Which I didn't want to say, because I didn't want to hurt your feelings. But the bottom line is, whose side is he on?

ASSISTANT

(to the YOUNG MAN) Oh, yours, Your Greatness, yours of course, under your leadership I'm sure we'll go far. Moron.

YOUNG MAN

Liar.

ASSISTANT

(to the PLAYWRIGHT) Tell the young man it's time to go?

PLAYWRIGHT

(to the ASSISTANT) So you can meet up with him in your room?

ASSISTANT

I wouldn't let him in the door.

PLAYWRIGHT

(to the YOUNG MAN) You want to go with him?

YOUNG MAN

I'm with you, man.

PLAYWRIGHT

(to the ASSISTANT) He's with me. You see? That's how it is. I might be an ugly, disingenuous old bastard, but he's with me. Leave us alone. I need a moment with my young man.

ASSISTANT

I'm not leaving the room.

PLAYWRIGHT

Just give me a moment.

> *The ASSISTANT rises and enters the bathroom slamming the door.*

The PLAYWRIGHT says nothing. After a moment.

What did he say?

YOUNG MAN

About getting with me?

PLAYWRIGHT

What did he say to you about me?

YOUNG MAN

About you? Oh, man, lots of shit, like that thing, "Say it's brilliant," like, about the play, like, before we went. And, like, coming down to his room and stuff, and that thing: "Oh, he can't get it up or whatever," which, who cares, right.

PLAYWRIGHT

No. I want to know did he say I was insane?

YOUNG MAN

Uh…. Sort of.

PLAYWRIGHT

What do you mean "sort of"?

YOUNG MAN

Well not "insane" insane. *(laughing)* Come on!

PLAYWRIGHT

It's nothing to laugh at.

YOUNG MAN

No, just, I mean, you're the smartest guy I ever met.

PLAYWRIGHT

It has nothing to do with that, my dear. Madness is not in the brain, it's in the blood. It can lie there sleeping, dormant, and then come on like a sudden fever. All you can do is pray that the angels will be there to transform the fever before it takes hold. To turn it into stories. Into magic.

YOUNG MAN

Yeah, man, I get that, I know what you mean. You're just freaked out that's all. You're just freaked out from that stuff in the paper. What you gotta do is you gotta start fighting back. Fight the bastards, that's what you gotta do.

The YOUNG MAN kneels at the PLAYWRIGHT's feet.

Look at who you are, man, that's your name on that book. All those people up there on that stage last night—that's you. That's magic. You do magic. You are magic. You're just letting the bastards bring you down.

PLAYWRIGHT
You are an angel.

YOUNG MAN
What it is now, man, is war.

PLAYWRIGHT
Maybe it is time for that.

YOUNG MAN
That's what we gotta do.

PLAYWRIGHT
Maybe it is indeed.

YOUNG MAN
War!

The ASSISTANT opens the bathroom door, he stands calmly in the doorway. He holds up a bottle of nasal spray.

ASSISTANT
Nasal spray?

PLAYWRIGHT
Yes. So?

ASSISTANT
You're up to that, are you?

(to the YOUNG MAN) Did you get him drugs?

The PLAYWRIGHT reaches for the nasal spay.

PLAYWRIGHT
There's no drugs. Give me that here.

The ASSISTANT holds it away from him.

ASSISTANT
Is that what you're up to?

PLAYWRIGHT
It was just in my toiletries, from before. What are you doing going through my things?

ASSISTANT
So you don't need it?

PLAYWRIGHT
I'm fine.

The ASSISTANT pockets the nasal spray.

Now let's get down to some war here, where's that phone?

ASSISTANT
The phone?

PLAYWRIGHT
That phone, the one with the speaker on it.

ASSISTANT
I took it back down to the desk yesterday.

PLAYWRIGHT
Well, then you call, then.

ASSISTANT
Call...?

PLAYWRIGHT
Yes, you call.

ASSISTANT
Whom?

PLAYWRIGHT
Call up the theatre, call that woman, that woman who works in the office, who handles the people, get her on the phone.

ASSISTANT
And say what?

PLAYWRIGHT
Tell her there's got to be some kind of opportunity for me to— She's got to set up some kind of interview with the paper.

(indicating the YOUNG MAN) He's right, you see, he's right. We're going to have us a war.

YOUNG MAN
Yeah!

PLAYWRIGHT
That's the way we've got to do it. We can't just let them talk that way. Do they understand who I am? Or for anyone, anyone deserves a rebuttal to slander.

YOUNG MAN
Right on!

ASSISTANT
I see.

PLAYWRIGHT
You get her on the phone.

ASSISTANT
Why don't I call her from my room.

PLAYWRIGHT
Yes, yes, that's good, you do that, you call her from your room.

The ASSISTANT heads out. The PLAYWRIGHT follows excitedly talking after him.

You call that woman. Tell her we've got lawyers, no, we've got better than lawyers, we've got American lawyers, you tell her that.

The ASSISTANT is gone.

YOUNG MAN
You think he's going to call?

PLAYWRIGHT
Yes he's going to call. Yes, yes, he's going to call. Of course he's going to call.

The YOUNG MAN approaches the PLAYWRIGHT.

YOUNG MAN
So we've got a few minutes yeah?

The PLAYWRIGHT shoos him away.

PLAYWRIGHT
No, get off me, leave me now.

Unperturbed, the YOUNG MAN sits at the desk and lays out a last line of cocaine from a small bag he takes from his pocket.

YOUNG MAN

You want to split this line?

PLAYWRIGHT

I'm good right now. I'm gonna need some more of that spray for my sinus. I've got sensitive sinus. My head gets all bogged up. You'll have to go for some more.

YOUNG MAN

Get it off him when he comes back.

PLAYWRIGHT

No no, you'll have to go get some, he'll know if I'm using that stuff, that I'm using this stuff. We'll keep this stuff just between us.

YOUNG MAN

I'll go after this line.

PLAYWRIGHT

Yes, fine then, I'm all right for a bit.

YOUNG MAN

You want to talk about my vehicle show.

PLAYWRIGHT

Not right now, no.

YOUNG MAN

You think he's going to call though, I don't think he's going to call. You should've made him call from here.

PLAYWRIGHT

No, no, he'll call. He's good, he does what he says he'll do. For me he will. He's good to me.

YOUNG MAN

Where did you get him from? Like an ad in the paper or something?

PLAYWRIGHT

I didn't "get" him, he got me. It was fate. A fated connection. Down home in Florida. I was in Florida. I was at a dinner one night and he was there, in the company of an older friend of mine. Not a friend really, more an acquaintance. Horrible man. And he was on a roster, at an agency, on a roster of young gentlemen, although being, I don't know, twenty-eight, what, twenty-nine, he was on the older edges of that business. And there we are at dinner and all night long he keeps looking at me, with this kind of Cheshire grin. Which is not the way, him an escort, his gentleman there beside him—well you know, you know where one in that arrangement should put one's attention— shouldn't be flirting with me. But then after I suppose enough drinks, I looked across the table and I said to him, "What are you thinking?" And he said, "I'm thinking, I wonder what I could get you to do for twenty dollars." Saucy! And he knew who I was, too. And talking like that right in front of his gentleman. Of course the old fart was pickled. They all were. But I wasn't. Neither was he. And later that night I took him outside to the parking lot, out back among the bougainvilleas, and I showed him what I'd do for twenty dollars. Oh, yes I did. And I never got my twenty dollars. And all these years later that's a funny we have, now and then I'll say to him, "You owe me twenty dollars." He gets a charge out of that.

(*laughs, then suddenly*) Goddamn my head!

YOUNG MAN
You wanna do half a line? I saved you half a line.

PLAYWRIGHT
No, no, you've got to get me some more of that spray—

YOUNG MAN
All right.

The YOUNG MAN does the last of the line on the desk.

PLAYWRIGHT
(*regarding the cocaine*) What are you doing? Don't be doing that out here. We don't want him coming back and seeing that.

YOUNG MAN
All right, all right, it's all gone.

PLAYWRIGHT
No, get that—clean that up—get that out of here. Get something to clean that up.

YOUNG MAN
It's no big deal, man.

PLAYWRIGHT

Keep all that business in the bathroom. Get something to clean all that up.

The YOUNG MAN heads into the bathroom.

YOUNG MAN

It's clean, man—whatever.

The PLAYWRIGHT pours himself a drink.

PLAYWRIGHT

I'm just saying there's a way things are done, that's all. And we're going to need more ice. You hear me? We're going to need more ice. Goddamn my head!

The ASSISTANT is standing in the doorway of the room, he wears an overcoat.

ASSISTANT

Headache pills aren't working?

PLAYWRIGHT

Oh. No. No, haven't kicked in yet. Or maybe I need some more.

ASSISTANT

Took all those pills already?

PLAYWRIGHT

No I got them all wet in there, dropped them on the—fell on the floor.

The YOUNG MAN comes out of the bathroom.

(*quickly to the YOUNG MAN*) Did you clean up all that, those pills on the floor?

YOUNG MAN

(*to the PLAYWRIGHT*) Yeah.

(*to the ASSISTANT*) What did the bastards say? You call them?

ASSISTANT

I called the theatre.

PLAYWRIGHT

Good, good, you called.

(*to the YOUNG MAN*) I told you he would.

ASSISTANT

I spoke with Diane—the woman in the office, the manager?

PLAYWRIGHT

Yes yes yes.

ASSISTANT

We had a good laugh. Robbie the designer told her about the other night here. Had a good laugh. She's a bit of a flirt herself. She invited me to dinner.

PLAYWRIGHT

Yes, fine, we can do that, maybe we can do that.

ASSISTANT

I said no.

PLAYWRIGHT

Well no exactly, why bother really.

YOUNG MAN

So what's the plan, man?

ASSISTANT

There's no plan. He knows that.

(to the PLAYWRIGHT) You know that.

PLAYWRIGHT

Yes well, yes I guess, yes.

YOUNG MAN

What about the war?

PLAYWRIGHT

Not right now.

The PLAYWRIGHT's head throbs, he presses his temple.

ASSISTANT

How's your headache? Maybe you could use some of this.

The ASSISTANT produces the bottle of nasal spray and tosses it on the bed. The PLAYWRIGHT immediately picks it up and snorts it. Holding a drink in one hand the PLAYWRIGHT expertly opens the bottle with his teeth and snorts the spray with his free hand.

I'm done. I am.

PLAYWRIGHT

Oh, all right, all right, it's not the end of the world, we're having a little party. Just once in a while's all right. It was just tonight.

ASSISTANT

(helpfully) Just *today*. It's today now. Then it'll be just tonight. Then it'll be just tomorrow.

YOUNG MAN

Man, tight-ass or what.

PLAYWRIGHT

(to the YOUNG MAN) Fuddy-duddy.

ASSISTANT

Diane in the office mentioned you picked up the rest of the royalty last night. In cash.

The PLAYWRIGHT says nothing.

Is there any of it left at all?

PLAYWRIGHT

We have money.

ASSISTANT

Not according to the bank.

PLAYWRIGHT

I'll be writing soon, I've got ideas, there'll be money coming in.

ASSISTANT

That's good. *(indicating the YOUNG MAN)* You'll need it to pay your staff.

YOUNG MAN

It's his money.

ASSISTANT

(to the YOUNG MAN) I may have been a fool but you're just stupid.

PLAYWRIGHT

Oh, settle down, have a drink.

(to the YOUNG MAN) Get him a drink.

YOUNG MAN

I wasn't so stupid when you wanted me to come to your room.

ASSISTANT

Intelligence had nothing to do with it, sweetheart.

The ASSISTANT moves to the window, throwing open the curtains.

Let's get a bit of daylight in here.

The room transforms, light of a cold, grey, rainy afternoon.

(to the YOUNG MAN) Now a few things you're going to need to know. His passport and plane ticket are in the desk there. The ticket's for New York but he'll only be there for a few days and he'll want to get to the house in Florida. But since it's the rainy season and the roof needs repair you'll probably be back in New York in a week. In terms of money, and it's mostly theoretical money, all the banking's in the valise there on the sofa, along with the schedule. Now, you'll want to check the schedule for some teaching dates he's got in the next few months. The important thing is he's got to be off the booze for at least three days before the teaching or you'll never get him in the classroom. Also, you'll want to be around to keep an eye on him when he's teaching to make sure he doesn't try to fuck the students, he's getting a bit of a reputation for that. Don't want to get blacklisted from the teaching 'cause that's where the money really comes from. Of course you'll have your show soon so it won't matter what trouble he gets up to then. The money will just be rolling in. But if the show doesn't pan out for you, you can just borrow some money from Warren Beatty. Oh, it's also important he's off the booze when he's teaching 'cause when he's drunk he tends to shit his pants, and that's not good for the "reputation," you know, for future engagements and all that.

PLAYWRIGHT

I guess this is necessary is it?

ASSISTANT

Just trying to get him up to speed, sir.

(to the YOUNG MAN) Oh, and he won't talk on the telephone, he thinks it's dirty.

(fake sotto voce) He's a bit weird like that.

PLAYWRIGHT

I've been a bad boy, have I? And this is my spanking?

ASSISTANT

You are what you are, sir. I'm off.

PLAYWRIGHT

Oh yeah, oh yeah.

The ASSISTANT takes a look at himself in the mirror near the door.

ASSISTANT

Long time since I really looked at myself in a mirror.

(into the mirror) What does it say in that play…? Something about broken dreams…. "A broken dream is worse than a forgotten dream." Maybe I'm lucky.

The ASSISTANT moves to head out.

PLAYWRIGHT

Hey now, hey.

The ASSISTANT stops and turns back.

You owe me twenty dollars.

The ASSISTANT takes a twenty from his pocket and throws it at the PLAYWRIGHT.

ASSISTANT

We're even. Cheers.

(to the YOUNG MAN) Good luck.

The ASSISTANT leaves. The YOUNG MAN watches him go.

PLAYWRIGHT

(calling after the ASSISTANT) Yeah yeah, I'll see you later.

The YOUNG MAN stands in the doorway, watching after the ASSISTANT.

YOUNG MAN

He's going, man, like, he's really going.

PLAYWRIGHT

Oh, please, hardly. My dear, in London he made it all the way to the airport. But he came back.

YOUNG MAN

He'll come back?

PLAYWRIGHT
Where would he go? Ah, he's drunk. He just can't handle his liquor. He'll be back. Oh, he's trying to make a point. He'll go off and find some diner where he can get a club sandwich with french-fried potatoes and a Dr. Pepper. *(laughing)* That's what he likes. Keep drinking maybe. Meet some rough fellow at one of those dark and dangerous establishments he likes so much. Oh, he's just pissy because of talk about your show. He was going to be an actor. Friend of mine put him in a show. Closed on opening night. Nineteen previews though. He never recovered. That's why he needs me.

The YOUNG MAN is watching at the window.

YOUNG MAN
There he goes, man, look, he's got, like, three suitcases.

PLAYWRIGHT
Come away from there, he'll be back, don't be silly.

The YOUNG MAN steps away from the window.

YOUNG MAN
What do you want to do?

(pulling on his pockets) Because I'm, like, totally out, that was my last bag.

The PLAYWRIGHT pulls several bags of white powder from his pocket.

PLAYWRIGHT
Oh, my dear boy, I am prepared, we are supplied to the end of forever.

YOUNG MAN
Right on!

PLAYWRIGHT
We're happy now?

YOUNG MAN
Yeah.

PLAYWRIGHT
All is right with the world.

SCENE TWO   Friday Night

The main light is the blue light from the parking lot outside the window. The YOUNG MAN sits in a chair, his legs up on another chair. The PLAYWRIGHT lies on the bed. Through the scene change we have been listening to the radio, and so are the two men. It is JULIE's review of the play which she reads on a radio program hosted by another woman, CAROLE.

JULIE

(*voice-over*) ...and when all is said and done I'd like to be able to say that this is a great play by a great playwright, but unfortunately I can't say that. Clearly a great playwright, but a great play? No. As the final scene played itself out at the opening last night, with his characters trapped in their world of discord and misery, I found myself hoping that this great man sees in his world more possibility of redemption than he does for his despairing and lost characters. I give it a rating of two and a half stars.

CAROLE

(*voice-over*) So not a recommendation?

JULIE

(*voice-over*) Well, Carole, that's the half star. I think it's an opportunity for people to see the work of a great man...

CAROLE

(*voice-over*) But not a great piece of work.

JULIE

(*voice-over*) Exactly.

CAROLE

(*voice-over*) So, Julie, why this play?

JULIE

(*voice-over*) That's my question. I mean it's an old play, a slight re-working of a failed play, I mean—

The PLAYWRIGHT gently turns off the radio.

After a silence.

PLAYWRIGHT

As a young man, it would wake me up. Pushing at me, tickling my face, whispering in my ear. It wouldn't let me sleep. And I wouldn't know what it was until I would rise, and I would set myself down at

my desk and let it pour out of my head, down my arm and through
my hand until my fingers were sore. And when it was done I would
wander from my bedroom into the moonlit night, down into the
fields below our house, into the grove of cottonwood trees. And
there I would be, finally spent. And, as if on cue, a breeze would
dance through the delicate boughs of those cottonwoods and their
tiny leaves would applaud my effort, my achievement, my gift. If
I could only hear that today, see the fluttering leaves reflected all
around me on the ground while the cool night air was filled with
the sound of nature's applause. That sound, that sound. Like the
icicle fingers of angels on a glass piano.

A silence.

Do you have any money?

YOUNG MAN
You're supposed to give me money, man.

A silence.

You don't have any money?

PLAYWRIGHT
He'll have money. You'll get your money when he comes back. He
always has a stash.

YOUNG MAN
I went through that stupid case in there, it's just papers and shit.

A silence.

You think he's coming back?

A silence.

Do you really know Warren Beatty?

A silence.

PLAYWRIGHT
I might go to Russia. They like me in Russia.

YOUNG MAN
Russia's fucking cold, man.

After a moment.

PLAYWRIGHT

That's true. Oh well. Fuck Russia.

A silence.

YOUNG MAN

See, the thing about me is I can't have nothing. Because I had nothing, right, totally nothing, nothing nothing. I gotta have something.

PLAYWRIGHT

You've got more than something, my dear. You've got what we all want. You've got youth and beauty.

YOUNG MAN

I'm twenty-eight years old and I'm fucking tired.

A moment.

Maybe my mother's right. She wants me to get a trade. Which is pretty funny right because I get a lot of "trade," doing what I do. But I know what I'm good at. And you gotta do what you're good at to get what you want.

A silence.

I'm probably gonna head out.

The YOUNG MAN does not rise.

PLAYWRIGHT

I think your mother is right, you should get a trade.

A moment.

Or maybe I should get a trade.

YOUNG MAN

You got a trade, you're a great man.

PLAYWRIGHT

Is that so?

YOUNG MAN

That's what they say on the radio. You're great.

PLAYWRIGHT

I think that's just the result of some kind of accident, or illness. Or madness.

YOUNG MAN

I don't know.

PLAYWRIGHT

But in actuality—in its manifestation—in reality greatness has no currency—it only really exists in the distance between where we think we are and what we think greatness is. It only really exists in its inaccessibility.

YOUNG MAN

(rising) I don't know. Anyway. I guess I'm going.

PLAYWRIGHT

"Flee flee, this sad hotel."

YOUNG MAN

Huh?

PLAYWRIGHT

A line from a poem.

YOUNG MAN

You really thing he's coming back, eh?

PLAYWRIGHT

Of course. And there now, you see, there you go. Perhaps there is true greatness. In compassion, in loyalty. In love.

YOUNG MAN

Yeah.

PLAYWRIGHT

Did you get me some of that spray?

YOUNG MAN

You've got some there.

Seeing the bottle at his side.

PLAYWRIGHT

Oh yeah, yeah.

The YOUNG MAN is at the door.

YOUNG MAN

You sure you gonna be okay or whatever? You got somebody you can call…. Or I mean somebody who can make a call for you?

PLAYWRIGHT
You're on your way out?

YOUNG MAN
Yeah.

PLAYWRIGHT
Shut the light when you go.

YOUNG MAN
Yeah. See ya.

PLAYWRIGHT
And here...

> *The PLAYWRIGHT takes the twenty the ASSISTANT gave him and offers it to the YOUNG MAN. The YOUNG MAN moves to take it then stops.*

YOUNG MAN
Oh, that's the.... That's the twenty he owed you. You keep that. He'll probably want it when he comes back.

> *The YOUNG MAN turns out the lamp and leaves.*

> *The PLAYWRIGHT is alone in the blue light from the window.*

> *He sits on the bed quietly, thinking. The blue light from the parking lot intensifies. Slowly the room is filled with the shadow of the bough of a great cottonwood tree. The PLAYWRIGHT sits up, alert. He looks up and addresses the audience. Slowly a sound begins, distant, faint.*

PLAYWRIGHT
The bedroom of a hotel suite in Vancouver, Canada, 1980. The best room in a fading downtown hotel. There is a door stage right which leads to the offstage sitting room and main hallway door. A king-sized bed takes up the centre of the room, to the left of the bed is a door to the partially visible bathroom. On the left wall is a large window which beyond the curtains looks out onto an unseen parking lot. Across the room, a mirror. The room aspires to a kind of grandeur which it manages when the lights are low enough, but when the lights are bright we see the ghosts of many sad nights lived here.

As the PLAYWRIGHT speaks, the sound grows closer, clearer. It is the sound of the icicle fingers of angels on a glass piano. The leaves of the cottonwood flutter in a kind of applause.

The stage is dark. It begins.

Blackout.

End.

Daniel MacIvor has been creating new theatre since 1986 and was for twenty years artistic director of da da kamera—an international touring company based in Toronto which he ran with Sherrie Johnson.

His published work includes: *See Bob Run, Never Swim Alone, Marion Bridge, You Are Here, In On It, How It Works* and *I Still Love You: Five Plays*, which won the Governor General's Literary Award for Drama in 2006. With Daniel Brooks he created the solo plays *House, Here Lies Henry, Monster* and *Cul-de-sac.* He works with theatres across Canada and the United States including New York's Montsgo Projects and Nova Scotia's Mulgrave Road Theatre, and he received an Obie and a GLAAD Award for his play *In On It* in 2002.

He has been writer-in-residence at the National Theatre School in Montreal, the University of Guelph, and was senior writer-in-residence at the Banff Playwrights Colony.

Also a filmmaker, he has written and directed the feature films "Past Perfect" and "Wilby Wonderful," and co-wrote and starred in "Whole New Thing."

Check out Daniel's web log at danielmacivor.com.